Spot and Discover
ANIMAL WORLD

William Potter

CONTENTS

Published in 2018 by **Windmill Books**, an Imprint of Rosen Publishing
29 East 21st Street, New York, NY 10010

Copyright © 2018 Windmill Books

Edited by Susannah Bailey | Written by William Potter | Illustrated by Ed Myer | Designed by Trudi Webb and Emma Randall

CATALOGING-IN-PUBLICATION DATA
Names: Potter, William.
Title: Animal world / William Potter.
Description: New York : Windmill Books, 2018. | Series: Spot and discover | Includes index.
Identifiers: LCCN ISBN 9781508193487 (pbk.) | ISBN 9781508193449 (library bound) |
ISBN 9781508193524 (6 pack)
Subjects: LCSH: Animals--Juvenile literature.
Classification: LCC QL49.P68 2018 | DDC 591--dc23

Manufactured in the United States of America

CPSIA Compliance Information: Batch BW18WM: For Further Information contact Rosen Publishing, New York, New York at 1-800-237-9932

Golden eagles
Keen-eyed eagles can spot their prey from 1.2 miles (2 km) away.

Find 5

Find 9

Bison
There were once 50 million bison roaming the American grassy plains.

GRASSLAND GRAZERS

The North American prairies are huge areas of grassland with few trees. Summers are dry and winters are very cold here.

Black-footed ferrets
This rare ferret will chase prairie dogs into their burrows.

Find 4

Find 9

Burrowing owls
These small owls lay their eggs in underground nests.

Find 10

Jackrabbits
Jackrabbits' long ears have been compared to donkeys' ears.

2

Find 4

Rattlesnakes
This venomous snake uses a rattle in its tail as a warning to keep away.

Find 4

Coyotes
These small wolves howl loudly at night to announce themselves to rival packs.

Find 7

Pronghorns
At just two days old, the speedy pronghorn can outrun a horse.

Find 10

American badgers
American badgers dig for prairie dogs and mice.

Find 4

Prairie dogs
Prairie dogs keep watch on mounds to guard their underground homes.

3

THE HEAT IS ON

Animals that live in the desert need to survive in extreme heat and cold, and to manage without water for long periods of time.

Spotted hyenas
These meat eaters are also known as laughing hyenas, for their whooping calls.

Find 6

Camels
One-humped camels can go for weeks without water.

Find 3

Fennec foxes
This small, large-eared fox has furry feet for walking on hot sand.

Find 3

Find 5

Oryxes
To save water, this antelope only sweats when its body is very hot.

Find 8

Ostriches
The ostrich is the largest living bird. It lays eggs 24 times the size of chickens' eggs.

4

Find 4

Addaxes
These rare antelopes have white coats in summer. These coats reflect the hot sun.

Find 7

Deathstalker scorpions
The sting from the tail of this scorpion is very painful.

Find 3

Monitor lizards
Large monitor lizards hibernate for half the year.

Find 5

Jerboas
The fast-hopping jerboa is active at night, feeding on seeds and leaves.

Find 13

Dung beetles
Dung beetles roll animal dung away to use as food.

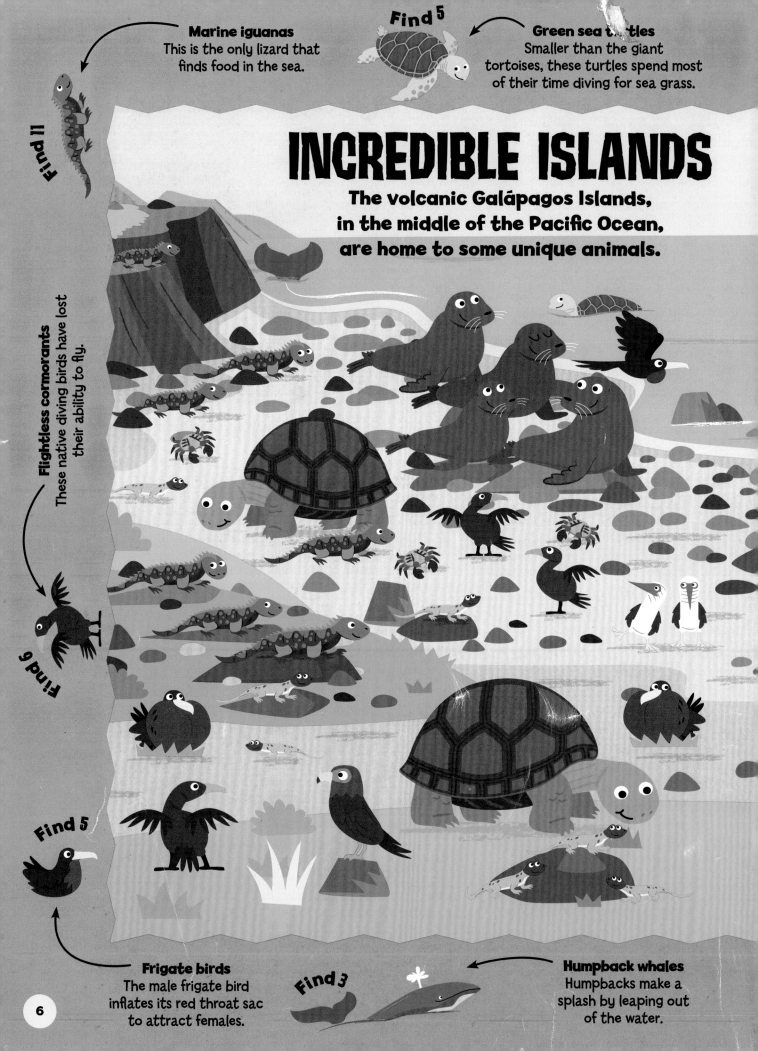

Marine iguanas
This is the only lizard that finds food in the sea.

Find 11

Find 5

Green sea turtles
Smaller than the giant tortoises, these turtles spend most of their time diving for sea grass.

INCREDIBLE ISLANDS
The volcanic Galápagos Islands, in the middle of the Pacific Ocean, are home to some unique animals.

Flightless cormorants
These native diving birds have lost their ability to fly.

Find 6

Find 5

Frigate birds
The male frigate bird inflates its red throat sac to attract females.

Find 3

Humpback whales
Humpbacks make a splash by leaping out of the water.

Find 11

Lava lizards
Eye-catching lava lizards bob up
and down to claim territory.

Find 4

Find 7

Sea lions
These playful sea lions like
company and often do tricks
in the water.

Find 4

Blue-footed boobies
This bright-footed bird dives
from a great height to catch
fish in the sea.

Find 6

Fur seals
Fur seals spend most
of their time out
of the water.

SUPER SAFARI

The Serengeti of East Africa is a land of grass and trees where large herds of animals graze.

Lions
The lion lives in a group called a pride. Lions hunt their prey as a team.

Find 9

Find 14

African elephants
This is the world's largest land animal. Each elephant herd is led by the oldest female.

Wildebeest
Over a million wildebeest roam the Serengeti, seeking fresh grass and water.

Find 12

Find 5

Cheetahs
The fastest land animal, the cheetah can sprint at up to 60 mph (100 kph).

Find 12

Baboons
Baboons live in large social groups, often grooming each other.

Find 9

Impalas
If this noisy antelope spots a lion, it will leap high and dash away.

Find 5

Black rhinos
This seriously endangered animal has two horns and very thick skin.

Find 11

Giraffes
The long-necked giraffe can eat leaves out of the reach of other animals.

Find 12

Crocodiles
The toothy crocodile has been around since the time of the dinosaurs.

Find 5

Zebras
Zebras follow the wildebeest and eat the dry grass that the wildebeest leave behind.

The Andes are the longest chain of mountains in the world. Most animals here have thick fur to keep them warm.

Llamas
Llamas are South American camels that have been trained to carry loads for farmers.

Find 5

Find 5

Condors
These vultures are the largest flying birds in the world.

Guanacos
When threatened, the guanaco will often spit.

Find 5

Find 9

Flamingos
Flamingos scoop up water with their bills to eat the tiny plants it contains.

Find 8

Guinea pigs
This rodent keeps its own nest but shares tunnels with other guinea pigs.

Find 1

Spectacled bear
South America's only native bear eats mostly plants and fruit.

Find 11

Chinchillas
Chinchillas are soft-furred rodents that live under rocks and in burrows.

Find 5

Mountain cats
Small, wild mountain cats live on the rocky slopes and hunt rodents.

Find 6

Pumas
These large hunting cats can live in high mountains, jungles, or deserts.

Find 8

Huemals
The stocky south Andean deer is built for climbing over the rocky ground.

11

Rhesus macaques
These fruit-eating monkeys are often found swimming in water.

Find9

Find 2

MANGROVE MOVERS

In the warm, flooded forests of India, the tiger is the king of the jungle, watching the animals that come to drink water on the muddy banks.

Asian elephants
Asian elephants have smaller ears than their African cousins.

Find 8

Find 7

Mongooses
Mongooses will fight cobras, as they're not hurt by the snake's venom.

Find 6

Wild boars
These wild pigs dig for food around the muddy banks.

Find 6

Fishing cats
Large fishing cats are good swimmers. They also catch fish from the water's edge.

Find 12

Chitals
These spotted deer form a large herd led by a female.

Find 8

Gharials
Gharials are crocodiles. They use their long, thin jaws to catch fish.

Find 4

Cobras
Cobras are long, hooded snakes that are highly venomous.

Pythons
These large snakes are good swimmers. They kill their prey by squeezing them.

Find 8

13

Arctic hares
The pale, winter fur of the Arctic hare helps it to hide in the snow.

Find 8

Find 9

Musk oxen
Muskoxen form a circle around their young to protect them from wolves.

FROZEN FIELDS
In the chilly north, many animals have thick white coats to keep them warm and to help hide them in the snow.

Wolves
This ancestor of the pet dog hunts in a pack.

Find 8

Find 8

Find 9

Arctic foxes
In summer, Arctic foxes swap their thick, white coats for thinner, darker ones.

Reindeer
Reindeer may travel thousands of miles a year in search of food.

14

Find 3

Snowy owls
With no trees here, owls make nests in hollows on the ground.

Find 11

Snow geese
The snow goose flies south to Mexico in the coldest months.

Find 6

Lemmings
Lemmings dig tunnels to find moss and herbs under the snow.

Find 3

Polar bears
These huge predators stalk seals and walruses from the shore and sea ice.

Find 4

Walruses
Walrus tusks on males can grow as long as human arms.

BAMBOO FORESTS

The cool mountains and bamboo jungle of central China are home to some very rare animals.

Clouded leopard
Although it's a good climber, this leopard hunts mostly from the ground.

Find 7

Giant pandas
Black-and-white giant panda bears eat almost nothing but bamboo.

Find 1

Golden pheasants
Beautiful, long-tailed pheasants peck for bugs on the forest floor.

Find 4

Find 2

Giant salamanders
These very rare creatures are the largest amphibians in the world.

Find 8

Sambars
Long-antlered sambars stamp their feet when surprised.

16

Find 13

Golden snub-nosed monkeys
These flat-faced monkeys live in a close family group.

Find 3

Red pandas
The cat-sized red panda spends its days in trees.

Find 8

Golden takins
This goat-antelope has an oily skin that acts like a raincoat.

Find 5

Crested ibises
There are only a few hundred of these very rare birds left in the wild.

Find 2

Temminck's tragopans
Male tragopans have red and blue "bibs" and horns. They use these to attract females.

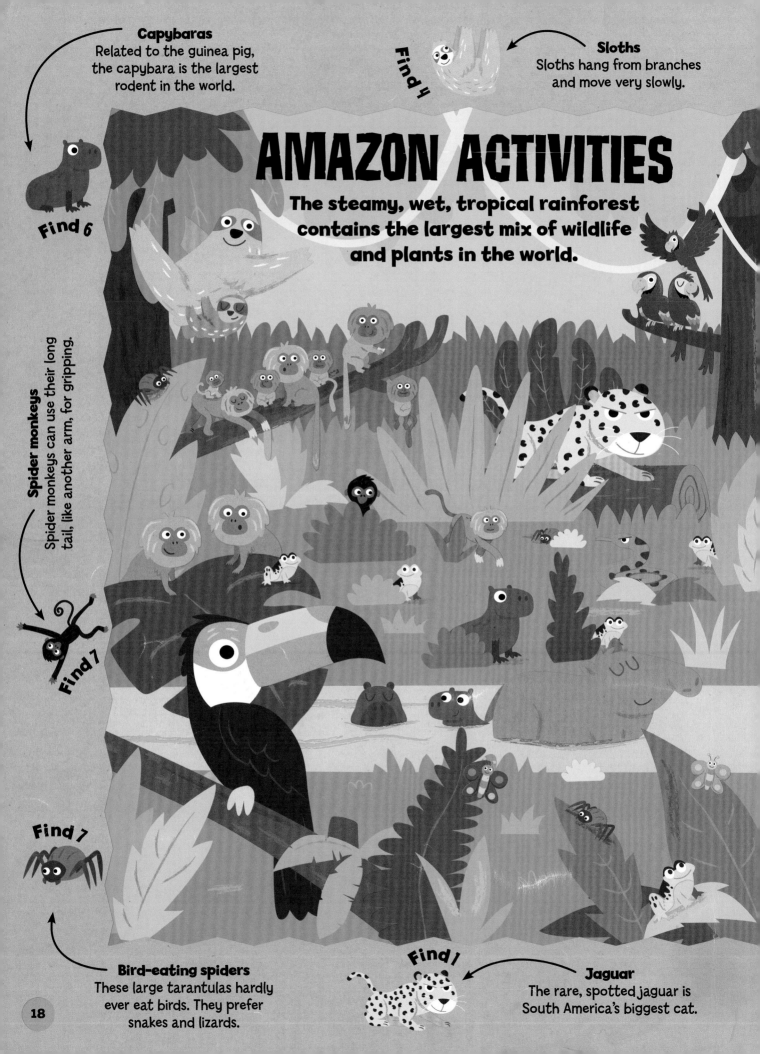

Capybaras
Related to the guinea pig, the capybara is the largest rodent in the world.

Find 6

Find 4

Sloths
Sloths hang from branches and move very slowly.

AMAZON ACTIVITIES
The steamy, wet, tropical rainforest contains the largest mix of wildlife and plants in the world.

Spider monkeys
Spider monkeys can use their long tail, like another arm, for gripping.

Find 7

Find 7

Bird-eating spiders
These large tarantulas hardly ever eat birds. They prefer snakes and lizards.

Find 1

Jaguar
The rare, spotted jaguar is South America's biggest cat.

18

Find 7

Macaws
This bright parrot has a large beak and long tail.

Golden lion tamarins
These small monkeys have orange hair around their heads, like lions' manes.

Find 11

Find 5

Toucans
Toucans use their large, hollow beaks to pluck and peel fruit.

Find 9

Tapirs
Tapirs feed on leaves and shoots, and are excellent swimmers.

Find 4

Poison dart frogs
The poison on this frog's skin was once used on arrow tips.

19

Malagasy giant rats
These large rodents can jump very high into the air.

Find 11

Find 5

Civits
Civits are nighttime hunters. They eat insects and steal birds' eggs.

AFTER DARK

In the Madagascan jungle, night is the time for hunters to come out. Their large eyes and sensitive ears help them find food in the dark.

Giant chameleons
A chameleon's tongue is longer than its body. It uses it to catch insects.

Find 7

Find 9

Flying foxes
Flying foxes are large bats that bite fruit to squeeze out the juice.

Find 4

Mouse lemurs
The mouse lemur is the world's smallest primate.

Find 5

Aye-ayes
The aye-aye has a long middle finger for plucking grubs from under tree bark.

Find 8

Geckos
Geckos catch flies. They have sticky feet for climbing up trees.

Find 6

Streaked tenrecs
This spiny worm eater looks like a mixture of a shrew and a hedgehog.

Find 3

Fossas
The fossa often climbs trees to catch its main prey, the lemur.

Find 2

Madagascar long-eared owls
These night hunters catch rats and small lemurs.

Answers

2-3 GRASSLAND GRAZERS

- Bison
- Golden eagles
- Black-footed ferrets
- Burrowing owls
- Jackrabbits
- American badgers
- Prairie dogs
- Pronghorns
- Coyotes
- Rattlesnakes

4-5 THE HEAT IS ON

- Camels
- Spotted hyenas
- Fennec foxes
- Oryxes
- Ostriches
- Dung beetles
- Jerboas
- Monitor lizards
- Deathstalker scorpions
- Addaxes

6-7 INCREDIBLE ISLANDS

- Green sea turtles
- Marine iguanas
- Flightless cormorants
- Frigate birds
- Humpback whales
- Blue-footed boobies
- Fur seals
- Sea lions
- Giant tortoises
- Lava lizards

8-9 SUPER SAFARI

- African elephants
- Lions
- Wildebeest
- Cheetahs
- Baboons
- Crocodiles
- Zebras
- Giraffes
- Black rhinos
- Impalas

10-11 THE HIGH ANDES

- Condors
- Llamas
- Guanacos
- Flamingos
- Guinea pigs
- Pumas
- Huemals
- Mountain cats
- Chinchillas
- Spectacled bear

Answers

12-13 MANGROVE MOVERS

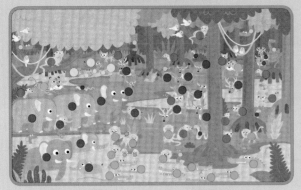

- Bengal tigers
- Rhesus macaques
- Asian elephants
- Mongooses
- Wild boars

- Pythons
- Cobras
- Gharials
- Chitals
- Fishing cats

14-15 FROZEN FIELDS

- Musk oxen
- Arctic hares
- Wolves
- Arctic foxes
- Reindeer

- Polar bears
- Walruses
- Lemmings
- Snow geese
- Snowy owls

16-17 BAMBOO FORESTS

- Giant pandas
- Clouded leopard
- Golden pheasants
- Giant salamanders
- Sambars
- Crested ibises
- Temminck's tragopans
- Golden takins
- Red pandas
- Golden snub-nosed monkeys

18-19 AMAZON ACTIVITIES

- Sloths
- Capybaras
- Spider monkeys
- Bird-eating spiders
- Jaguar

- Tapirs
- Poison dart frogs
- Toucans
- Golden lion tamarins
- Macaws

20-21 AFTER DARK

- Civits
- Malagasy giant rats
- Giant chameleons
- Flying foxes
- Mouse lemurs

- Fossas
- Madagascar long-eared owls
- Streaked tenrecs
- Geckos
- Aye-ayes

Glossary

burrow An animal's home, made of underground tunnels.

endangered An animal that is threatened with extinction (when there are no more of one species left).

grooming Cleaning another animal's fur or skin.

herd A large group of animals.

native Coming from a particular place.

prairie Grassland.

prey An animal that is hunted by other animals.

unique One of a kind.

venomous Poisonous.

volcanic On, or coming from, a volcano.

Further Information

BOOKS

Amazing Animal Journeys by Chris Packham, Egmont, 2016.

Animal Kingdom (The World in Infographics) by Jon Richards and Ed Simkins, Wayland, 2014.

Animals by Camilla de la Bedoyere, QED Publishing, 2014.

The Animal Book, DK Children, 2013.

WEBSITES

For web resources related to the subject of this book, go to: **www.windmillbooks.com/weblinks** and select this book's title.

Index